By the same author
Casanova: The Man Who Really Loved Women
(Penguin Books)
Freud: An Intellectual Biography (Other Press)

THE
FINAL
REMINDER

How I emptied my parents' house

Lydia Flem

Translated from the French by Elfreda Powell

SOUVENIR PRESS

First published in English, 2005, by Souvenir Press Ltd
43 Great Russell Street, London WC1B 3PD

Translated from the French
Comment j'ai vide la maison de mes parents
Published by Editions du Seuil 2004

This paperback edition 2007

ISBN 0285637827
      9780285637825

Typeset by FiSH Books, London

Printed by MPG Books, Bodmin, Cornwall

A mother's death must be something very unique, unlike anything else, and must awaken inconceivable emotions within us

Sigmund Freud
Letter to Max Eitingon
1 December 1929

For me, this book has another significance, a subjective significance that I realised only when the work was finished. I could see then that it was a piece of self-analysis, my reaction to my father's death, the most important event, and the most heartrending loss in a man's life

Sigmund Freud
The Interpretation of Dreams
Preface, 1908

Contents

Emotional Storm

A Nothing,
That is what we were, we are and
shall remain, undying:
The Rose of the Void, the
Rose that belongs to No one.

Paul Celan

No matter what age we are, the day will come
when we find ourselves orphaned, without father
or mother. Although childhood is long gone, this
double loss does not spare us any the less. If it has
not already happened, it is there waiting for us in
the future. We knew that it was inevitable, but,
like our own death, it seemed far away, in fact
unimaginable. Long buried in our consciousness
by the course of our daily lives, by our refusal to
acknowledge it, by our wish to see our parents

last for ever always at our side, their death – even when we are forewarned by illness or old age – always takes us by surprise and leaves us dumbstruck. This ordeal which we have to confront and overcome occurs twice, but not in the same way. When our first parent dies, the survivor is still there. We feel pangs of anguish. There is bitter, perhaps inconsolable pain, but when the second disappears, we are left without a family. The parental couple are together again in their grave, but we are separated from them definitively. Oedipus gouges out his eyes, Narcissus weeps.

It may be that the bonds of marriage and friendship are no less powerful than the bonds of filiation, and quite possibly much happier, but it still means that after our grandparents' death and then our parents', there is no longer anyone behind us. Only a double absence, like a terrible chill in the back. When our parents pass on, they take a part of ourselves with them. The early chapters of our life are finished. We have to supervise the burial of the people who transmitted life to us, our creators, the first witnesses of our existence. As we lay them in their graves, we are also burying our childhood.

How can we live without communicating this double grief to anyone, a grief that rocks and undermines us with its sudden arousal of violent feelings? How many of us feel carried away on waves of often unutterably shameful emotions? How can we dare tell anyone of this jumble of feelings that invades us, this chaos of anger, oppressiveness, infinite sadness, unreality, revolt, remorse and strange freedom?

Whom can we tell of this storm of passionate feelings, that are so confused that they cannot be named and remain nameless, because in our disarray and discomfort we find them totally loathsome?

How can we not feel despicable when we are invaded with anger, bitterness and even hatred towards this dead person? Is it quite normal to experience a frightening impression of abandonment, emptiness, of being torn away, and simultaneously, or perhaps later, a will to live that is more powerful than our sadness, a blind, triumphant joy in having survived the strange co-existence of life and death?

How many children – even ourselves perhaps – owe their conception to a strong desire to fight death and the pain of grief, with the pleasures of love? Who dare evoke the shameless almost maniacal sense of celebration we sometimes feel, that heightens our senses, sharpens our appetite, increases our consumption. Each of us, in our own particular way, finds ourselves transfixed, invaded, swept away by an emotional storm that we must face, alone.

Some react by distancing themselves from everyone, like a wounded animal licking its sores; time cures nothing, but attenuates the suffering, but sometimes the suffering encysts and forms a wound that can never heal. Others throw themselves into activity, living in a whirl of agitation about thousands of mundane worries, problems to be sorted, debts to be settled, goods to be managed, tearing up or settling accounts with other siblings. Some become bogged down in ritual, gestures, etiquette, the savoir-faire of bereavement, the order in which things should be done, dark colours, the correct phrasing for the circumstances; but they do not show what they are experiencing: their anger, indifference, the lack of emotion, the silent weeping of a small child, the bitterness and hopelessness of never having been valued, recognised, loved, and, now, of no longer being able to hope for these things either. Others, however, find a path of forgiveness and create a new bond beyond death.

Reconciling ourselves with the dead, attaining a serene memory of them can only come with the slow passing of time. One by one the seasons must pass, and life, step by step, gesture by gesture, will hold sway over death. If we can pass through the tempest of feelings, without excluding any, however acute and vile they seem, if we can give our consent to whatever feelings arise, a feeling of lightness will burst into bud, a rebirth after the flood, a springtime of our self. Even if, in a part of ourselves, this double loss remains irreparable and shocking.

In years gone by, death was an experience that lived in the heart of the community; religion and custom dictated gestures, sustained the grief-stricken, but today bereavement has to be carried out in the lonely compartment of our private life. Each one of us buries our dead, mumbling personal ceremonies, and hurriedly effaces our loss in social life: no more black or crêpe, no more outpourings or tears, nothing solemn, no exterior sign of unhappiness, scarcely a day off work, and life takes up its course again. It is in solitude that we each find ourselves alone. No longer is there anyone to accompany us from those first moments when we are plunged into grief. Grief is not shared.

Over the long months, the difficult years which often precede parents' deaths there is no open exchange either. Their old age, their illnesses, the slow or rapid decline of their health, of their capacity to think or make judgements, their loss of autonomy, their sufferings – those that they endured themselves and those that they inflicted on their family, or sometimes on their partner – all that is silent. It is a subject upon which we avoid embarking, for we are ashamed.

How can we recount the distress, the indignation, lassitude, incomprehension, grief that were provoked in us by their incoherence, their unfairness in that moment they teetered into a second childhood and wanted to make us their parents, yet at the same time keep an unshakable hold? Are we betraying them by mentioning this? Are we touching an ancient taboo by revealing our parents' nakedness, like one of Noah's sons?

Distraught and overwhelmed, we modestly avert our gaze and seek to hide that almost obscene part of the end of our parents' life. We each do what we can to get through this testing time, cobbling our own precarious, unhappy, conflicting path, and say nothing.

Working in the Void

Freud, who survived his mother by barely nine years, did not have to empty his parents' home, since his sister Dolfi lived in the family apartment until the Second World War and deportation. Had he had to gauge the extent of it, Freud might perhaps have spoken of this terrifying yet liberating *work in the void*, which obliges us to confront old ghosts, turning us back into cannibal babies, full of greed and covetousness for our parents' riches, into creatures who harbour grudges and demands, obsessively seeking to control the passage from full to empty, into heartless adolescents wanting to jettison everything, and in their frenzy of empowerment wanting only to forget their parents and wipe out the past, into adults who still want to accomplish their pious filial duty conscientiously, but encounter cumbersome ghosts at every turn.

So even when we have just lost our second parent, almost immediately we must go through one of the most painful experiences there is, the most onerous tasks imaginable, redolent with a multitude of contradictory affects. This is the task of emptying our parents' house. At the same time, in the same place, in the same act, all at once all our emotions become jumbled. It is a time of intense catharsis. Anguish and despondency. Vexation and happiness. Pain and jubilation.

I find the word 'emptying' offensive. I would prefer 'arranging' or 'clearing up', but this is only part of the work. Yes, we do have to sort out, evaluate, classify, order, pack up, but we also have to select, give, throw away, sell, keep, and in the final analysis, save, if one is living in the same place from one generation to the next, where the strata of the past have accumulated, then we truly have a responsibility to 'empty' the parents' house.

'Emptying' has a sinister resonance; like pillaging a tomb, stealing secrets from the Kingdom of the Dead – the curse of the pyramids – it makes us sound like robbers, stealing goods from corpses.

It would be good if we could soften the word, weaken its brutality, tone it down, say 'clear' instead, or even, perhaps, 'close' as we say of a holiday home at the end of summer. But, if this is leave-taking, then it is a final leave-taking, there will be no return to these holidays.

Like it or not, there is a somewhat indecent element of aggression in life. The passage from one generation to the next – the one ascending, the other descending – 'The king is dead, long live the king' – is not without a hint of symbolic murder. Each of us, not just in fantasy, kills his or her parent, both parents even, since we survive them.

A revolting thought, but in the course of things, we see those who witnessed our birth die, and we bury those who put us into the world. We never know our parents' childhood and youth, and they will never know the last years of our life, just as we shall never know our children's. We are born into our parents' family, we die in the family we have created. So, yes, when we in turn mount the throne, it is because we have become the survivors. Surviving our children is intolerable. Surviving our parents is natural, but nevertheless difficult.

It is what is known in psychoanalysis as the Reality Principle, the slow and inevitable work of bereavement which begins with an over-investment in the dead parent before we progressively lose interest in favour of life.

But first there is the feeling of loss. For a long time yet it will be impossible to resolve the idea that this loss is definitive, irreversible. The child in us revolts at this. What we are mourning is not only a cherished human being, but love itself. The feeling of security, the background canvas on which we sketch our life. We ask ourselves: is it our fault, perhaps, that the person now gone is not there, perhaps we have unconsciously killed him/her through our greedy, aggressive fantasies?

So how do we make a void of our parents' house without feeling terribly guilty of draining everything from it that we had hoped to possess in some very old dream, in some flashback of our unconscious? How can we carry away – for real, and with the strange authority of the law – everything that has been taboo until now? How can it be that, in one radical sweep, inheritance gives us the authority to seize for ourselves what only a few hours before was not ours, and to obtain from it the most total unrestricted, blameless enjoyment? How can we enter those places that were never ours, never since our birth – until now? Why can we now in all impunity take, throw away, destroy from there if we think it best? What is it that has changed in us? Nothing, and everything.

Inheriting is not the same as receiving a gift, a reward, a compliment, a reassurance, or help. Inheriting is in no way receiving a gift from my parents. It is exactly the opposite.

Becoming the owner by way of succession is not the same as taking something that is offered: it is legally taking possession of goods, obtaining usage of them without them being willed to us by the testator.

The verb 'to inherit' is the opposite of the verb 'to be bequeathed'. To give under a Will signifies an explicit wish, a choice, an act. Inheritance is the opposite of a legacy, it does not presuppose any wish, does not translate an intention towards us. The law undertakes to circulate goods which, if it did not, would be neglected. They are, by default, attributed to the legal inheritors who are determined, or sought, by a lawyer. In France this law is known as the Notoriety Act. This has nothing to do with reputation in the sense of celebrity, but is an acknowledged, manifest, public act, by which an inheritor is shown not to be an impostor but the person to whom an inheritance is destined through filiation.

So, the law has declared me legal inheritor, but I still feel like an impostor. How can I receive things that have not been given to me? When they were alive my parents never offered me this pretty oriental rug which I coveted. Why have I the right to it now that they are dead? They never wanted to give it to me as a gift, so how can I take it without having the feeling of forcing their hand, of abusing, robbing them even?

The law of succession is specific. It says that the deceased has made no deposition of last wishes known to this day. This is where fantasy and reality enter into collusion. In their Will, my dead parents would have made known to me an old wish made prior to their demise. Without any declaration on their part, how can I be sure of their consent? Did they really want me to enjoy their possessions? What does it mean to 'not receive' parents' possessions, but to find oneself the possessor of them in spite of oneself, in spite of them?

'Emptying my parents' house' sounds so frightful because it is precisely this expression that touches an unconscious truth.

The law does not reflect a state of mind; it cannot be ambivalent. What the law imposes, language forbids or makes nuances in it, or makes it more complex. My French dictionary takes into account our intimacy, our internal debates, our hesitations:

> **To empty** *(transitive verb)* the act of rendering a container empty, of removing from a place, of expelling, causing to flee. Its opposite: to fill, refill.

Clearing my parents' house of its furniture, like a sinister bailiff. Taking away what was in their drawers, their cupboards, like a thief. Scattering the linen, crockery, clothes, papers, traces of their life, like a looter. In emptying their house, isn't it rather my parents that I am clearing away, the way one removes entrails from a fish or a chicken?

Associations resound with those of the language: emptying, voiding, gutting. Emptying also means clearing, closing down, exhausting, putting an end to. Terribly aggressive connotations. Is it unbearable to talk about them, write them down? How it is that this task that each and everyone of us will have to undertake some day or other (unless we have brothers or sisters who take on the responsibility in our stead) carries such a burden of violence that we would prefer not to breathe a word to anyone about it?

Am I wrong in persisting in writing these pages, this book which discloses that part of ourselves that we would rather keep secret? Or, on the other hand, is it worth trying to approach this burdensome silence that we carry within us by using words? Like a dangerous abscess that needs lancing, opening, piercing, in fact emptying. Isn't there an expression, 'emptying our heart'?

Emptying is a solace. Is it unseemly to say this? Yes, our dear departed, we have loved them tenderly, but it is now our turn to empty them, to empty the place of them, the way we chase away an intruder or a bad dream.

Does this sound too violent?

Shall I be pursued by ghostly upholders of the law who will ask me for accounts, invading my nights with nightmares as an act of retaliation? Or is it the way of inner deliverance, the now-or-never of closing one's childhood? Of voiding a disagreement, a quarrel.

Emptying is also making a void within oneself, unveiling oneself, unmasking oneself, abandoning oneself.

Journeying to the void is a difficult moment, as if one is leapfrogging the void.

AD1313. *Vuider un dit*: 'pronouncing a judgement'. Bringing about the end of an affair, putting to rights, resolving, terminating.

So, time to go for it. Time to settle the question. Time to tell what cannot be told. As in a story, I shall begin in the past.

On the Marches of Death

I write your name
On absence without desire
On naked loneliness
On the marches of death:
'Freedom'.

Paul Eluard (1942)

First of all I felt shameless. I had to disregard all the rules about discretion: rifling in personal papers, looking in handbags, opening and reading correspondence that had not been addressed to me. Transgressing the elementary rules of politeness, flouting those who taught them to me was wounding. Being indiscreet was alien to me. I had never gone through anyone's pockets, or plundered secret drawers, even less opened a letter that was not addressed to me. But the authorities have no modesty; in the hours that followed my mother's death they demanded documents which obliged me to ferret every-where, to invade her privacy, open files, consult statements of accounts, diaries, in order to find documents or information needed by the State, Social Security, the lawyer, the cemetery.

My greatest act of shamelessness was that I had to make an official declaration that the woman who had carried me in her womb was dead.

I had to alert relatives, telephone the family, friends, utter the unspeakable words: how should I phrase them? I have something sad to tell you. Very sad. I'm very sorry (in a muted, broken tone of voice that transmitted the truth before the words themselves spoke the irrepara-ble). She had been ill for several months with three periods in intensive care, she had returned from London with bad bronchitis. With the world turned upside-down, I heard myself consoling the people I was calling; I took their grief upon myself, I tried to soften it, to find ways to console them. No, she had not suffered, she died in my arms, I kissed her brow, stroked her face and held her hand. M. held her other hand. Yes, I had taken her home from the hospital as she had wished. She died in her own bed, surrounded by her nearest and dearest. She went out like a little candle.

Had I forgotten anyone? I consulted her address book, turned the pages, exhausted with emotion. How do we find the strength to make one telephone call after another, to say the same words over and over again, giving flesh to her death now that the first few hours have passed, making the event float in a sort of protective unreality, a no-man's-land of consciousness? Perhaps I was only an automaton activated by an unknown hand that forced me to do what I did without thinking about it, all those small symbolic acts, like writing the announcement for the deaths column, choosing words, names, respecting the delay in publication, counting the lines, checking to see if the post had arrived on time, buying the newspaper to see where the announcement had appeared, making sure there were no unfortunate misprints . . .

I went through the motions but it wasn't real. Deep down inside me, a small accusing voice was asking me whether by doing this I was killing her? You say that she's dead, but it's not true. I answered it rather uncertainly, worn down by an old feeling of guilt that would not go away, that I had not dreamed it, that she had died in my arms, that I had seen her breathing slow down and peter out until the last breath, that I had closed her eyelids over her beautiful brown eyes, that I had touched her still warm skin and lifted the duvet from her chest against which I had snuggled in times past and which now no longer moved.

Yet, it is was true, the transition from life to death is so fine, so subtle, in fact so simple, but also so truly incomprehensible, that several hours later, seeing her lying in bed resting against the many cushions we had slipped under her head, I thought I saw her move.

The fear of looking at her, dead, of being present at her death, had not affected me; she had asked me, made me promise that I would be with her, I was ready, I was not going to abandon her in the sterile anonymity of a hospital room. I had not been able to accompany my father on his final journey. He was in intensive care after some problems with his health due to the very rare side-effects of his medication. I was beside him before he was plunged into an artificial coma to try to save him by giving him artificial respiration. For a whole month I had gone to sit by his bedside, stroke his cheeks and hands, still feeling the familiar contact of his fingers, of the signet ring on the last phalanx of his little finger, that was slightly too short and bent like mine.

It was our most subtle sign of mutual recognition. We had this small physical anomaly in common which we both laughed about, but which we were proud of because it formed a bond between us through a bodily similarity that was much less visible than eye colour or hair texture. It was our secret bond, a complicity between father and daughter that had no need for words to express it.

My father died without knowing that he was dying. We never said goodbye. Was that better or worse for him? How can we know? Every human being takes a part of the mystery away with him. Perhaps he died with the elegance and reserved discretion that were part of his personality in life. He had suddenly disappeared, it was as though he had evaporated, in two days, without being a burden on those who loved him, without even offering a few words to his daughter, who would have loved to hear them.

Perhaps, without wishing, my father had given me the opportunity to find the words myself that he was unable to give me. An infinitely precious gift, like the hollow of an intaglio. I had never thought of it in this way. I was angered by his silences, I found my personal effects quite inadequate to go out into the vast world without him. Two years after his death, which seemed less like a decease than a disappearance, a cruel and infinitely painful evanescence, I began to feel a sort of gentle sweetness within me.

Before burning out like a candle, breathless, my mother had murmured her wish to meet my father again. She expected me to watch over her to make her departure more gentle: I was there. I hoped that in these final moments she would grant me what she had always denied me – this was the power to satisfy her, to give her pleasure, the permission to respond to her expectation without being criticised by her, without her acerbic comments, without her tripping me up at the last moment, simply the possibility of experiencing her tenderness with no ulterior motive.

As I gave her a daughterly kiss on her brow and cheek, repeating words of tenderness in her ear, I thought that throughout my whole life I had tried to please her, that I had always hoped to receive unconditional love from her, but in vain.

Only at that moment of losing her, at that very last moment, she showed that she was satisfied with her daughter, she had nothing more to reproach her for, she accepted my hand in hers, my lips on her skin, my words in her ear.

For once, just for once, she was happy with me. She welcomed me for what I was. She had confidence in me.

This was a strange experience for I did not know if the feeling of consolation would prevail over the sadness. I could not rejoice in that moment of appeasement between us, since it was the last, but was I going to be angry with her for the rest of my life? Our rows, our misunderstandings, our mutual incomprehension had lasted long enough. A peace treaty had to be signed. The fact that she was on her deathbed did not matter. In her inflexible will to live my mother had often repeated to me that every cloud had a silver lining. Could it be that she herself suffered from being eternally dissatisfied, perhaps she never realised the measure of her scathing words, of her tone that brooked no reply, of her devastating comments. In her clumsy way, she loved me after her fashion.

Mourning her, experiencing the emptiness brought tears but, more than anything else, the pain of exposure. While we may not already have realised it, this is the last occasion we can measure our parents' limitations, witness their fragility. After all, they are but poor human beings.

The idea of not having failed in my duty, of having brought my mother home so that she could die in my arms, according to her final wishes, relieved my distress, gave me the strength to confront all those painful tasks that still had to be done.

At her burial I read one of her favourite poems: Paul Eluard's 'Freedom'.

Ground Zero

It was a strange paradox: everything I had dreamed of in my childhood and adolescence, that I had longed to be given, that I had hoped for, coveted and asked for unsuccessfully, or which I had been forbidden to touch ('You've two left hands. I don't want you to break it'), everything that I had been prevented from using or wearing ('You're not careful enough') had suddenly become mine.

My feelings and those of my parents were of no account any more. Hope, covetousness, tears or anger were no longer met with reticence and refusal: the law had made a decision for us. 'The sole, unique legal inheritor' was what the lawyer said, everything was passed on to me. In bulk. In all the disorder and confusion of my feelings.

Whatever I had longed to possess in the past, everything that displeased me now, everything that I found a burden, that had come to me too late or too soon, everything that I did not know what to do with, that upset me: it was all mine now. Through inheritance.

I no longer wanted anything. I lacked all desire. I was numb.

How could I receive what was not given to me, with their hands, of their own free will, with their good intent? Why take these things home with me if they had not confided them to me when they were alive? Being an orphan is inheriting, so the law says in a weighty nutshell, which does not stand to reason. Can we take without conquering? Can we accept what was formerly refused us? How could I not feel a frightful inner feeling of revenge now that I carried away the footstool that my mother never wanted me to have? Why did I have to feel this miserable emotion 'in the name of the law'? If I did not want to keep a particular lamp, or table which they cherished, had I the right to get rid of it? Was the little black silk camisole wrapped in gift paper intended for me? Was I the inheritor of it, the intended receiver, or the usurper? Were these things already mine, or were they still hers?

A sensation of emptiness, of oppression made

me feel hollow inside. As the 'sole and unique inheritor' legally I had nothing to share with anyone, but I felt a pressing need to give, to offer. Was it to unburden myself, offload myself to escape from this suffocating situation behind closed doors, alone with my parents? I was an only child, with no brother or sister, older or younger. That was how it was in their lifetime and so it would remain after their departure. I had become a solitary orphan. A solitary heiress. The only gift that I wanted to receive had been their trust. I wished that they had given me an absolute, unshakable, total trust, long before they died.

So what importance did these bits of property, these foreign objects, these partnerless memories have? Were they refused to me, or was I refusing them? Their old magic was extinguished, it no longer worked. I felt hostile to 'all that' at that moment. What was the value of this trinket, this scarf, this watercolour that my parents had never made me a gift of, of this dictionary which would have been useful for my children, which they had deemed not good enough to give me, of this flask they could have given me with a smile and that I now received unsmiling.

I am all for donation and against inheritance. People should always make a Will, detailing by name what they would like to bequeath and to whom it is destined. The passing down from one generation to the next should not be done wordlessly, it should be a choice, an offering, an explicit, concerted, reflected transmission, and not just a convention, a passive laisser-faire resignation. I inherited, but I would have liked to receive.

An insistent question weighed on my mind. What should I do with the contents of their house, with this and with that? Was I really free to choose? The law offered me full ownership of a world that was still theirs.

For each object, each piece of furniture, each garment, each document, there were but four directions, like a crossroads, or a compass rose: I could keep, I could give away, I could sell or I could throw away. Each time that my eye or hand considered any object, a choice had to be made. How many things does a house harbour from the attic to the cellar, how many decisions would I have to make? Dozens, hundreds, thousands of times, I would have to evaluate an object and decide its fate: whether it should go into the dustbin, to be taken away, given away, negotiated over…but it was the 'undecided' or 'to be decided later' categories that proved to be the most important. The status quo largely prevailed over the four categories prescribed by common sense. I felt infinitely discouraged, overwhelmed by the house.

In the early days I persuaded myself to 'clear up' rather than 'empty' my parents' house. Several times I would say one word for the other.

Putting in order or emptying of furniture often proves to be a testing experience, but these banal activities became unbearable when they, as on this occasion, stirred up my parents' past life, at each moment I had to confront their loss, their disappearance: why, I would ask myself, am I at their house when they are not here?

The dead do not disappear from our memory. We can evoke them at will; they continue to exist within us; but on the other hand they can no longer think of us. The dialogue is entirely in our imagination. We cease to exist for them. But now we try to imagine what they would have thought had they been here. Would they have approved of our decisions? Am I respecting their wishes?

Would they have been shocked to learn that I had no wish to live in their house? In my heart of hearts I told myself, as an encouragement, that there had been nothing to prevent them from leaving precise instructions had they wanted to, and that, that not being the case, I must act as I wished.

Nevertheless my father and mother remained in me. Nothing in reality could now contradict the images that I kept of them, those that I would invent for myself, and the memories that I would reconstruct in their likeness. They were mine, they were within me. My feelings were a mixture of serenity and violence. I thought of my nearest and dearest: there was no longer anyone behind me, only beside and in front of me. I now occupied the position of the elderly one, the one on whom people could count, the one who had created a new lineage.

Looking at everything around me made me dizzy.

In cowardly fashion, I put off resolving this dilemma till later. I chose to begin with taking away a few knick-knacks, a few books which had belonged to me since adolescence and I had always omitted to take to my house, as if it were reassuring to know that they remained in the family home like a final bond with the past, a guarantee that separation was not entirely consummated, that I could always return there to find refuge. Then I decided to take the presents that I had given them.

In childhood disputes it was always said that giving is giving, taking back is stealing. Was I a thief? Could I shamelessly take back the two volumes of Jacques Prévert's poems in the Pléiade edition, the fruit bowl brought back from New York, the catalogue of a Modigliani exhibition in Venice (how heavy it had been as I lugged it up and down the steps of the canal bridges), the Tuscan pot that they had never really liked?

Nothing was simple. Each object spoke of their absence, revived the loss, the loneliness. The task crushed me, the house was too full, the distress too fresh. I recoiled. I felt an immense weight weighing me down. I wanted to run away, desert the place. Idiot, I thought to myself. Forget your scruples. Your parents poisoned you enough while they were alive, why go on poisoning yourself after their death? Do whatever you want.

I went up to the attic. In a corner was a completely round black felt cushion, decorated with a smiling face, big red lips, astonished eyes, two big gold earrings sewn on to the ears, it was the cushion from my bed when I was a child, my darling Bamboula. I held it tightly against myself as I used to do, then put it back where I had found it.

The telephone rang. I lifted the receiver, someone spoke my mother's name, asked if they could speak to her, hear her news, she didn't know, she had confused our voices.

No, I said, this isn't her, this is her daughter, and I gave my name instead of hers. She was not here, she would never be here.

Before leaving the house, I went into their bedroom. Everything was there, intact.

On a bedside table on my mother's side was a portrait of my father, leaning on his elbows beside an open window, a handsome young man who had been smiling for fifty-seven years. Beside him, faded with time, was a picture in which, in the foreground, in a forest of black and white faces, were my mother's and mine. It was a photo taken in New York in 1972 – on top of one of the Twin Towers.

Ground Zero.

Nothing and Too Much

There is something sacred about the parental home. Tampering with it has a hint of sacrilege, profanity.

Where should I begin the dismemberment? How can I summon the courage to sweep away the uniqueness and coherence that belongs to this place? By clearing one room at a time, but which one? Is there one room that is less imprinted with memories than the others? The lustre of life radiates everywhere. There is not a corner or cranny of the house that does not carry the vibrant traces of its departed inhabitants. Where shall the devastation begin? Where shall I begin to vandalise? Does a gentle approach exist? I run my hands over objects, I take one, stroke it, put it back, take up another but I can make no decision to seal its fate. Shall I attack the kitchen, the drawing-room, the living room? Despoiling, dispersing, separating. Why does disorder and desolation have to be added to my grieving?

Things are not just things, they bear human traces, they prolong the memory of people for us. In their modest, loyal way, objects that have long accompanied us are no less faithful than the animals and plants around us. Each has its history and a significance that has melded with that of the people who used and loved it. Objects and people together form a sort of unity that cannot be painlessly separated. I wandered through the house, irresolute, overwhelmed, powerless.

Since I had to bring things to a close, I decided to take away any personal papers – without looking at them. I would sort them later, taking my time, giving them the attention and time that I did not have in those early moments of bereavement.

I transformed my garage into a place for archives. I put up yards and yards of book shelving, ranged the boxes, files, folders that they themselves had kept over the years, letters and souvenirs side by side with bank statements, telephone and electricity bills, insurance premiums and duplicates of tax returns. They had kept everything, absolutely everything for thirty, forty, sometimes even fifty years or more. I should have to spend hundreds of long rainy winter evenings going through all this mass of paper, for without looking at them properly, it was difficult to decide if they were important or not, whether to keep or to sling them.

Most important were the rows of folders, files and documents that my mother had collected to compile her double family tree, as well as some bits about my father's family. It was an immense job that she had accomplished with patient care, a taste for order and a desire for perfection: which were all qualities she possessed.

Did I have to become the archivist of their lives? Turn my house into a museum of their past? An altar to the ancestors? If it were healthy to keep a powerful bond with one's roots, didn't it become dangerous when they pushed their way out of the earth and invaded the aerial part of the tree, to the point of suffocation.

I was twenty when my mother got it into her head to start her genealogical researches. I watched her doing it with a certain amount of irony. Her zeal annoyed me. I would have preferred her to talk to me about her own past when she escaped genocide, rather than about some distant ancestor who was possibly a musician in Napoleon's army. While she was overjoyed to make the acquaintance of her ancestors, she was not aware that filiation was not self-evident in her descendents. Every genocide breaks the evidence of the succession of generations, She was seeking her ancestors, yet I had no access to my own mother's history.

In the first months of her wild enthusiasm, she had dragged my father and me into the peaceful cemeteries that lay between the Rhine and the Mosel, where she piously noted down all the inscriptions she could decipher on the preserved graves of her ancestors. While I preferred climbing trees or sitting on some stone to pursue another '*Recherche*'. I was deep into Proust's novel. In the midst of the graveyard stellae, this reading provided me with imaginary ancestors, and opened a way of escape from the uninterrupted pursuit of 500,000 generations before us...

My mother had never had time to put her genealogy into shape though she had traced it back to the seventeenth century. Nevertheless at the end of her life especially she had written down the memories of her early childhood for her granddaughter. It was a happy childhood in the 1920s, between Cologne where she was born, and the countryside beside the Rhine. In spite of my insistence and encouragement she never went beyond her arrival in Strasbourg after Hitler's rise to power in 1933, and her joy in discovering a country where Liberty, Equality, Fraternity could be written in capital letters on the front of the town hall.

I suspected that my father had prevented her from writing about her experiences in the concentration camp. He had wanted to spare her, he said, of very strong emotions, or was he protecting himself? She respected the ban until her brief widowhood. I knew that she had, like him, agreed to speak to future generations and that they had made some audio-visual cassettes of several hours of interview on their memories as old escapees of Nazi camps, funded by a university foundation.

They had never offered to show me these eye-witness accounts and I had not felt that I had a right to ask to see them. The silence that we could not break, neither they nor I, lasted after their death.

It would be down to me to break this taboo, on my own. I wondered if what they had hidden from me was worse than what I had read or understood? What I knew was that I could not know. They had not wished me to know. It was forbidden knowledge. Sullied with horror, shame, denial, a knowledge trapped in ice, petrified.

My parents had fought to survive; the children of the generation after the genocide, as I was, had to fight to live in their own right. In order to live your own history, you had to extract yourself from the crushing, undifferentiated jumble of their traumatised history.

Trying to unglue your own psyche from your parents' involved interminable self-analysis..

Why, among so many other possible items, did I take it into my head to open this tiny leather suit-case, shiny with age? Chance or intuition? It contained bundles of letters that I never knew existed. Written in German by my father's mother and addressed to him when he was at boarding school and still only a very young adolescent in 1938, these letters spoke of a time that my father had never mentioned in my presence.

Of this Russian grandmother who was deported and murdered by the Nazis in 1942, I knew nothing. For years I kept a small photo of her in my address book; she was holding a little kitten up to her face and smiling at it, with a gently amused expression, her hair held in a chignon and with high, pronounced cheekbones. Very Slav. On the back were pencilled the words: 'Scheveningen, 1939'.

With her a whole world had disappeared: the Russian family, Russian cooking, Russian language, Russian memories, Russian names. I would love to have known her, but my father very rarely mentioned her, as if speaking about her was painful. When would my father have seen his mother for the last time? When did he learn of her appalling death? As a child I had often tried to accompany her into the gas chamber, imagining myself as a prisoner, panicking, wildly distressed about the fate reserved for her children, asphyxiated, suffocating, seized with terror, blotted out.

What had my father kept of his mother? A bundle of letters, one or two photographs, some of her characteristics perhaps, the shape of her face. And a small jewel, that his elder brother kept to give him after the war, a blue enamelled medallion that I would have liked to wear, but which was refused me, I don't know why. All I received was her first name, Rose. It was too heavy a legacy.

Hovering between melancholy and bitterness, sadness and pain, gratitude and discouragement, I thought that at least I had had the chance to see my parents grow old and now be able to gather together the objects that spoke to me of them. My parents had wanted to keep everything. They had been unable to detach themselves from anything, could throw nothing away, because their own youth had been shattered by too many exiles and disappearances. They burdened me with too much, because they had too little. They sought to fill their void.

From one generation to another, nothingness weighs you down, as excess also does. Do we only ever pass on what is negative?

Like an Apple on a Goat

In the pantry, behind stacks of fish kettles, couscous pans, copper saucepans for jam-making, sauté pans, fondue dishes, dozens of empty jam jars and marmalade pots, stocks of mineral water, stewed apple, carrots and peas, rolls of tissue paper, bits of string, bottles of wine and various oils, I discovered, as innocent as newborn babes, my very first feeding-bottles.

How could my parents – people whom I believed to be full of common sense – have thought it necessary, or amusing, or of spiritual value, or daft, or... to keep these small thick glass bottles with old brown rubber teats? A lot of babies had passed through their arms since they had fed me with milk, had they not understood, then, that these feeding bottles were no longer of any use and it was absolutely pointless to keep them? Had they been expecting me to keep them, indefinitely and in vain – since I had breastfed my daughter and my one attempt to make her use a feeding bottle had come to an abrupt end the moment I sterilised them and forgot them on the stove and the nauseous smell of the wizened teats in the bottom of the dried-out saucepan hit me.

I took the old pots of jam that I had found beside the unbelievable dairy relics to give away, and left the pantry, exhausted, full of doubt, dumbfounded.

There is nothing we can be indifferent to in our parents' house.

A few days later, I was back on the attack, sorting bank papers, telephone bills, various prospectuses, instruction books for various household appliances or makes of hi-fi, which filled several drawers. And here, once again, concealed within peaceful and boring covers of well-ordered files and folders, lay the unexpected. Some intruders had slipped in among the ordinary household papers, carefully arranged in chronological order, and these came from an epoch that had long passed. The 1950s made a sudden appearance. Here, without warning, were receipts from the time of my birth – for rent that my maternal grandmother had paid for 20 rue Delécluze in the Kremlin-Bicêtre [a small village outside Paris]. It was all written in detail: Rent – 4.431, half-yearly surcharge – 341; rubbish collection – 430, water – 289, electricity – 94 and most importantly, baths – 277 . . .

Still in a state of stupefaction I discovered next an envelope containing other bills dating from the same period. Among them was one for my mother's confinement in the maternity ward where I was born. Everything was there: the price of the room from 15 to 23 July, the cost of medication, daily care, the rent of the delivery room, forceps, telephone calls, and even boarding for the baby. Held together with a paper clip were also the invoices for the time I spent, on my own, in the maternity ward until 5 September. My mother had had tuberculosis. The doctors thought it would be a good idea to take her newborn baby from her for eight weeks to protect it from the Koch bacillus.

I had been told vaguely about this early separation, but I had never had any idea of the length of time involved and I shall never know the repercussions.

How does a baby feel when entrusted to hospital personnel rather than to its mother? I had thought for a long time that that could not have made the beginning of my life easy nor the early relationship between myself and my mother. To convince me otherwise I was shown a photograph taken at the clinic, in which I lay in the arms of a very pretty nurse, overprinted with a reflection of my young father, moved by tenderness, smiling at his baby behind the glass partition of the room. Now I know this room's number – 466 – the price of the breast milk with which I was being fed and the cost of the chest x-ray that I was given fifteen days after I was born. The name of the paediatrician was Maurice and the invoice was made out to 'The Infant Flem Lydia'.

Before leaving the house – I had made a rule that on each visit I should take away something in order to dispel the overwhelming sense of discouragement I felt when I thought of that whole world I had to disperse, a world trembling with nostalgia and vaster than an ocean that had to be emptied spoonful by spoonful – on that particular evening I took home with me a painting that was full of colour and tenderness and I hung it in my hallway. It would welcome me home just as it had welcomed them home. Its title, painted below the upper border, to which I had never paid any attention was: *My past is like an apple on a goat.* What it depicted was indeed a very gentle-looking goat, advancing with a red apple on its back, towards a melancholy figure which I had never been able to decide if it was a woman or a man or a double human figure, a sort of hermaphrodite or a couple, a man and woman combined. In the background was a little dancing village, like one of Chagall's pictures: the church, houses, windows all topsy-turvy. In the night I went downstairs with a flashlight to look at the picture. In the darkness it glowed red and luminous. This double figure wore a wide skirt like a Russian peasant's, with very white round breasts beneath a décolleté blouse and two strange arms which came out of its belly, like two erect penises, fingers held open towards the malicious goat with triangular hooves. The picture was redolent with joy born of despair. It suited me very well, translating as it did this mixture of wrenching separation and freedom, that was so difficult to endure.

At the Bedside

I write what I cannot say to anyone.
Primo Levi

I was dispersing the things they had loved, whether they were chosen with care or haphazardly, whether they had been kept out of habit or because 'you never know...', kept as markers to preserve significant features of life, or shut away in pockets of forgetfulness, or protected from time's depredations in order to witness their existence. What right did I have to them? How was it not possible to feel guilty, forcing my way into their intimacy, entering their room without knocking, unmasking their little ways or their grand gestures, their eccentricities, their wounds, of breaking and entering that part of themselves that they themselves did not even glimpse and which was now revealed to me with impunity. An underlying question nagged me constantly: Were there family secrets? What was I going to discover that I wanted or did not want to learn? Dare I open all these drawers, read all the papers, read between the lines, or was I going to turn my back modestly on certain matters, bury them in sacks and boxes without broaching them, throw them away or even burn them without ever knowing?

How could the unseemliness of such an indiscretion be resolved even when it was coupled with old buried desires that dated right back to childhood: listening at doors, peeping through the keyhole, picking up noises from my parents' bedroom, satisfying a curiosity, known to be forbidden since the beginning of time, and yet legitimate: how did my birth come about? From what love-making was I conceived? From what desire to survive? What unconscious characteristics had my parents in their turn passed on to me? From what unthinkable maternal and paternal event was I the issue? How was I to be inscribed in a lineage that was weighed down with the dead who had gone up in smoke, families massacred with complete impunity? How could I be the daughter of orphaned parents, slaves put to hard labour, human beings whom they wanted to subtract from the human race, reduced to silence for so long by the deafening silence of the whole world? How could I inherit from parents who had made me a safeguard against horror? I was not their child, but their shield against the world.

Against this inexpressible past, to this succession of traumatic events that they lived through before my birth, what could I pit except obstinate research, in which I was feeling my way with lost words. To become their 'free' inheritor, I would have to break the absoluteness of a silence to which I had always been hostage. Writing became urgent.

Through the concoction of language, the unspeakable fact of their past would no longer prevent me from living my life, separate from theirs. I would no longer be the passive shelter for their distress and their silence, but the active inheritor of my filiation: 'In order to possess what you have inherited from your forefathers, you must acquire it.'

As I came home from their house loaded down with numerous bags, suitcases, files and a lamp that my father had designed and made in the 1970s, I sat down at my work table and wrote down several notes at random in a kind of state of excitement that acted as a barrage against the many feelings that were invading me. These were feelings that were difficult to formulate out loud: feelings that lay between pain and deliverance.

My mother's death so soon after my father's brought them terribly close to me, obsessively close even.

They occupied all my thoughts, all my actions. Not only in my mind but also in practical terms. I could not stop evaluating and deepening every aspect of my ties with them over the years. It was a concentration of psychic exploration.

I reread some of the letters I had written them, surrendering to the task with a sincerity that they had never echoed towards me. They had a touching naïveté which I now found unnerving and made me ashamed. I would have preferred not to recognise myself in this immodest mirror, in this long-held illusion of transparency.

I had too many words to say about my parents

who had none, and this disparity justified my writing, but it returned me to the dizzying loneliness I had experienced in their presence.

The distress I felt was even more intense in that it was a duplicate of their own distress, although they had not been able to confront it, elaborate it, digest it, metamorphose it, only try to restrain it, keep it at a distance for better or for worse. I had grown up unable to lean on them, sponging up their anxieties and their nightmares, without anything ever being expressed in words. Perhaps they were not even aware of it.

Quite the reverse: we went about our ways as though we were an ordinary little family: papa, mama, the maid and me, when in reality it was: Hitler, Stalin, History and us. It's just possible this could be a subject for discussion devoid of any emotion, but never a meeting point, even a hesitant one, across words and emotions, a conversation between parents and child. What haunted their nights and their bodies, especially their poor degraded mutilated tortured bodies, violated in the unspeakable 'down there', they both, one and the other, sought to bury in an impossible oblivion. Their bodies spoke in their place with stomach pains, difficulties in breathing, insomnia, stress, backache, dreams of torture, heart-breaking cries in the night. Close to theirs, my body was in their image, imprinted by the war.

I took refuge in books, music, painting, dance. I sought in art and literature the expression of sensations and feelings that wandered through the house like elusive ghosts. My parents encouraged me in it, even looking for a rapport, which isolated me even more. They were taken in, I had yielded to their demons and made them my own. Our lives had telescoped into each other's. My mother had not been gassed in Auschwitz, but I had always lived as though I were suffocating.

A sombre inheritance.

While their tongues had remained silent, their papers spoke volumes. I had a vital need to read their archives, to consult them in the flesh. To be exact about dates, note the facts, look at the truth like a reality, not just a terrifying ghost, beyond meaning.

There was a moving and testing symmetry: in a drawer of odds and ends by my father's side of the bed, I saw buried under some old small coins, watches and other bits and pieces from his pockets, his official number as a political prisoner of war. In another part of the house, a few minutes later, I came across a Nazi book, *Der Weg zum Reich*, that at the time of Liberation, my father had found thrown away on a bench in the train coming back and in which he wrote the only confidence I had ever read from his hand:

Souvenir of the final days of the 'grand Reich'. Found this book in a carriage on the Wülzburg-Brussels line. 15 May 1945. The most beautiful journey I have ever made.

I wanted to know. I no longer wanted to be a passive vessel of such great pain, but to assume the history that had preceded my birth, to understand the atmosphere into which I had been born. I wanted to release myself from a past that had remained trapped in their lungs and had prevented me from breathing freely. The documents that I had gleaned here and there in various parts of the house established the raw but clear and distinct facts, without any shadow of emotion, without the risk of a deadly meltdown.

My father was arrested as a Russian on 7 March 1942 at the University of Charleroi, in Belgium, 'as a hostage', a police report specified. He was eighteen years old. Until 26 April 1945, he spent thirty-eight months in a Wültzburg labour camp in the fortress of Weissenburg in Bavaria. In his papers I also discovered a photograph taken at roll call in the camp yard, and his prisoner's identity card at the Lager: Ilag XIII. On the photo you could see him holding a board with the number 334 chalked on it.

Here he was, a very young man with a long melancholy face, fine pale features and abundant dark hair. He was wearing round spectacles which make him look like a poet or an anarchist. He did not look tired but rather absent, as if he wanted to appear impenetrable to the enemy, emptied of emotion, turned inward. Perhaps he constructed a hiding-place within himself to elude the powerlessness of his situation, to escape from the prison of terrible reality. Perhaps, after he had been freed, he had never left this shelter, this intimate prison, which had saved him but which yet clung persistently to his skin.

Of his incarceration he had only ever told me

tragi-comic anecdotes, of the cat he managed to trap and eat with a friend, which he claimed tasted of rabbit, the wooden toys he made in secret in the workshop which he exchanged for bread at Christmastime, when the German guards returned to the village to see their children and wanted to take them presents, the war notwithstanding. He remembered a taciturn prisoner who was the brother of Trotsky's assassin. He gave his stories a touch of humour and adventure which made them more thrilling than frightening to me. Of fear, hunger, humiliation, he said nothing.

During my childhood, his Russian friends would come to our house for the evening, they would laugh, speak three or four languages at the same time, listen to Slav music and eat borscht and zakuskis, drink vodka with their smoked fish. They dared not return to their homeland for fear that the Soviet authorities would force them to stay there. Later I dreamed that I had assassinated Brezhnev to free my ancestors' country. A strange dream of the accomplishment of desire: I had stuck a needle into his nose and as he was dying he turned into an old *babushka*.

Remembering my paternal grandparents was loaded with pain and drama. Both of them had been murdered. They had no grave, nor house to empty. Nothing. There was no place to gather in their memory. No archives, photographs, no trace of their lives. I did not know where they were born, or had lived, had loved each other. Of them nothing remained, not even a pair of spectacles or a hat, just a void. My father had inherited nothing.

On my mother's side of the bed the small locker drawer contained, among the usual detritus of family life – crumpled handkerchiefs, half-used medicaments, reminders, keys etc. – three small flat boxes in which lay her French decorations: the cross of a Voluntary Combatant of the French Resistance, the Deportation Medal for Acts of Resistance and the Combatant's Cross.

As a child I could not understand that a mother, a woman, had military medals. I was proud of the fact and disturbed by it. How could my mother be attractive and military? Wasn't the order of the sexes turned upside-down? And how could I rebel against or lose my temper with a heroine, a Resistance worker, a victim of barbarity, without feeling thrown into the oppressors', the torturers' camp?

On the cards that accompanied the decorations, I read the dates that I have never been able to memorise, never inscribe within myself.

My mother had been deported to Auschwitz on 11 August 1944 and had remained there until 29 May 1945. She was twenty-three years old when she was arrested in Grenoble on 10 July 1944. A Resistance recruit had blundered by giving her a rendez-vous in a cul-de-sac; tortured by the Gestapo, the young man had betrayed his contact, the Germans were waiting for my mother at the appointed time: 'You're in for it now, little girl'. She had held out under torture for as long as it took her mother and friends in the Resistance to go into hiding. The danger, the sang-froid, her age and her will- power to fight to live were the factors to which my mother attributed her survival in Auschwitz. And notably one extraordinary detail. On the day of her arrest, she happened to have in her pocket a Red Cross badge that she had found lying on the ground the day before. This badge saved her life – when she arrived at the camp she was able to claim that she was a nurse.

Several days later when I was tidying her desk, among the writing paper, stamps, tissue-lined envelopes, rolls of Sellotape, visiting cards and letters awaiting a reply, I found a unique document: slipped into a plastic sleeve, preciously kept, the small scrap of paper on which she had scribbled a few words in pencil to her nearest relatives to reassure them of her fate. This little slip of precarious life had been written in Convoy no. 78 which left Lyons on 11 August 1944 with about 650 people, on train no. 14166, made up of nine wagons, which crossed France through Mâcon, Chalon-sur-Saône, Chaumont, Vittel, Epinal and Belfort, and arrived in Auschwitz on 22 August 1944. The small torn strip of paper, she gave furtively to a member of the Red Cross asking them kindly to forward it to her family or to her neighbours at Tours. A friend kept it without knowing if she would ever see the person who had written it again. In firm handwriting, my mother had pencilled these words:

14 August at Chaumont. We are on our way East, since we are not able to go to Paris.

Morale is good. I feel courage. I hope that we shall see each other again soon. The Red Cross has great style. I kiss you all. Edith.

Innocent Incest

Those few words torn from a Death Convoy in Chaumont station and placed in the hands of a stranger lay before me, saved from chaos and oblivion, found again by a survivor, a revenant.

I slipped this small piece of her presence into a file to join the other remnants that had escaped from the mass of papers that emerged from all corners of the house, like a crowd forming on the day of a demonstration. It seemed to me that I could hear these voices of the past crying out, as if they wanted me to listen to them all, so as not to forget a single one. They pressed around me, surrounded me like the sirens' bewitching threnody murmuring in my ear: Remember me!

From every nook and cranny more and more sheaves of paper also emerged: envelopes, cards, notes, notebooks, small diaries, photocopies, photographs, maps, rough drafts, lists, reminders. They made me dizzy.

Should I, out of fidelity, keep these frail fragments of life? Was I enslaved to them? My father and mother had perhaps unconsciously sought to bury the horror under an abundance of the anecdotal, of the ordinary, of little bits of happiness extracted from life, as and when the need arose. It is always this sort of thing that defies the enemy. Everyone has these piles of paper, kept intentionally or haphazardly, or through laziness or lassitude. My parents had kept almost every layer of their lives, everything they could save from the void: was it an imaginary shield against the void that lived within them? And how did that concern me at present? I had not envisaged that becoming their heir would turn me into their psychoanalyst. I was torn between a desire to pursue my exploration and an increasingly powerful desire to get rid of everything. But curiosity still prevented me from doing so.

Like an obsessive investigator, a Sherlock Holmes or a Miss Marple, searching the crime scene, it would not have been very complicated to reconstruct their activities and goings-on from ten or twenty sparse clues. I could retrace their movements across the world, their holidays, their purchases, their leisure activities, their tastes: diaries that had accumulated with the passing of time, aeroplane and train tickets, car itineraries, restaurant and hotel bills, museum entrance tickets, theatre programmes, travel brochures, town plans, postcards, leaflets from interesting places to visit. More sombre and disquieting were their medical records kept meticulously by my mother over the years with lists of medications, x-rays, notes on a car accident containing the medical evidence gathered on the occasion of a court case against the other party (a well-heeled woman in a sports car who had already killed a pedestrian in a previous accident, and was now guilty for a second time of jumping a red light and throwing my mother and her small light Italian car against the front of a house), etc.

On a lighter note there were the plans for our house (and also all the sketches that had preceded them, the bills detailing its construction, the model etc.), press cuttings on all and everything, notes taken on language courses, at conferences, correspondence, invitations, greetings cards, diplomas, instruction manuals, advertisements, telegrams... overflowing from shoeboxes, folders, paper envelopes, plastic envelopes, leather envelopes, letters and post-cards from the entire globe and still more letters, often mine obviously.

Found again when I was unprepared for them, ten, twenty, thirty years after I had written them, they were painful to reread but no less painful to throw away after I had read them. This unchosen confrontation with myself was at first moving, but it soon became a burden. I wanted to cry out: Enough! Enough!

After a long, too long a time spent wondering whether I had the right to destroy anything they had not themselves thrown into the wastepaper basket, after turning old out-of-date papers over and over in my hands, I was overwhelmed by a furious wish to throw them away. It was like a garden that had become a jungle, and the joy of chopping, pruning, cutting down to the quick, arose within me. I yielded to this desire to create a void. I hurriedly threw all these tired bits of paper into huge bins that became so heavy that I could not lift them, in just the same way that memory refuses to be extinguished by oblivion.

From the massacre I saved just a few gentle words from my father to my mother, with his teasing drawings of the sun, cows, birds or lovers with the nicknames he had given them just after they met and had always remained: Pieps and Paps.

But finding a piece of paper covered with their handwriting filled me with nostalgia. Writing, like a voice, is an emanation of the body. But while the voice is extinguished, writing remains.

The line of their downstrokes, the upstrokes of their consonants, the curves of their vowels encapsulated their presence, gave an intensity to their absence. I could no longer touch or look at their living faces, but I could still run my fingers over their familiar writing – this was not dead.

I slipped the letters, cards, documents which bore witness to their history into transparent folders. I put them in chronological order. Their lives were drawn. Do we all swear that we will write our parents' story? Even after their death, do we ever stop living for them, through them, according to them, contrary to them? Is it a debt that pursues us for ever?

Over the years the brandings of the dramas of war grew fainter, life went on in a gentle, benevolent way. Then in the final years the memory of the past once again became immediate. Both wanted to write their eye-witness accounts before disappearing so that future generations could not claim: 'We did not know'.

They had wanted to trace their 'disappeared', to make enquiries to verify the dates of their deportation, the number of the convoy that had taken them to death camps, to have their names inscribed on commemorative monuments, on the walls of names, the data bases, so that each dead person could find their identity again, their individuality, their humanity. This was no insignificant duty on their part but a final battle for memory.

Among the papers they had collected and preserved to hand down to me was a letter from the Netherlands Red Cross which announced to my father on 10 November 1949 that his mother, born on 23 September 1879, had been captured in Holland and deported to Auschwitz. According to a German list, entitled *Judentransport aus den Niederlanden* and dated 2 September 1942, where her name appeared on page 44 beside the number 1089. 'As most of the deportees were gassed [*vergast* in Dutch] immediately and burnt in the crematoriums [*gecremeerd*]', the director of the Netherlands Red Cross wrote that Mme 'Rosa Widenski-Flem most likely died on 5 November 1942'.

This declaration written on headed Red Cross notepaper was her only grave.

A letter from the Centre of Contemporary Jewish Documentation, dated 11 January 1999, told me that, according to my mother's wishes, the members of her family deported from France had been inscribed in Volume IV of the Book of Remembrance, held in the crypt of the Memorial, where each year a ceremony was performed dedicated to the victims of the Shoah who had no grave. I had never known this. She had never told me either that most of her family had been deported from French soil. My grandmother, who was saved by the nuns of the Convent of Notre-Dame-de-Sion, near Grenoble, had never spoken of her mother either, nor of her sister, her brothers and sisters-in-law, who had perished, murdered by the Nazis. Was it that I had not been able to hear it, or that they had not wanted me to know?

As I learned of this listing, I welcomed them and lost them at the same time. Though they had disappeared in smoke in the clouds in the sky over Upper Silesia, thinking about them brought them back to earth. They found their place again as dead human beings among living ones.

> *Friedrich Kaufmann*, a maternal great uncle, born 30 June 1898 in Cologne, deported from Drancy to Auschwitz in Convoy no. 33 on 16 September 1942;
>
> *Bertha Kaufmann*, my great grandmother, born 24 August 1860 at Oberembt (Germany) and her daughter *Irene*, born on 18 November 1893 at Jülich, deported from Drancy to Auschwitz on Convoy no. 45 on 11 November 1942;
>
> *Julius Kaufmann*, my great uncle, born on 17 November 1899 at Jülich and his wife *Ruth*, born on 4 December 1908 at Brema, deported from Drancy to Auschwitz on Convoy no. 47 on 11 February 1943.

The dead no longer floated round me like threatening ghosts. The dead, even when they had been atrociously murdered, became dead. I ceased to be the small child who imagined herself padlocked inside the gas chamber and withheld her breath so as not to inhale the poison and die.

Is it brought home enough to the children of survivors of genocide, in Rwanda, Cambodia, Armenia or elsewhere, that it needs time for their dead to become dead, and for the survivors to become living among the living?

When I was a small child and my mother had brought to a close all her attempts to tell me of the unbelievable horror that she had seen and lived through in the extermination camps with 'One can never put into words what we went through, it's impossible to talk about it,' I was run through with a sensation of boundless impotence. My father ordered my mother to turn towards the future, not to seek out memories, and to stop talking about 'all that'. They left me alone with the effect of these unfinished words. They could not measure the resonance of their silent distress. Had they forgotten that even very young children try to understand what they hear and want to discover the hidden meaning of what is being concealed from them?

My poor childish imagination tried to fill in the blanks in their accounts, tried to picture for myself what was so terrible that my mother had lived through. My mother, that is to say, my mother's body, the body of the woman who had carried me in her womb, who had held me in her arms, on her knees, whose skin I could always smell and touch. What had happened to this skin that was so soft and perfumed, what had happened to that tender bosom, to those loving arms? How could I enjoy this maternal tenderness, as I approached a body that had been beaten, shaved, tattooed, starved, humiliated and whose disappearance had been premeditated on an industrial scale.

My body was not yet completely distinct from hers. The evocation of violence, torture, physical cruelty perpetrated on my mother's body blended with my sensory experience of that milky skin, that warm breath, those gentle looks and made bodily proximity disquieting and pervaded with sadistic sexual fantasies that hovered on the edge of my consciousness. No precise image swept through me but a diffuse sensation of danger, the perception of an obscure murky connection between sex and death. This terror invaded my curiosity about sexual matters. Everything, desire and the acutest kind of anguish mingled together.

At night strange nightmarish ideas came to me. My body would be run through with sudden emotions that I could not recognise as my own. The primal body-to-body of mother and child was loaded with unbearable images. How could I escape from it? Where could I find refuge? In whom could I confide? My parents had neither confided me to the world nor protected me from all my inner dreads. Innocent incest.

Several weeks after my mother's death and two years after my father was buried, I could read the words that put an end to the alienation that silence had imposed, to the fantastical closeness that was too strong.

Dare I write it here? When I lost my parents, I also lost those terribly anguishing, paralysing identifications. When they left me, they freed me from their silent hold over me. At last I would be able to withstand them.

Female Inheritance

As I was going through drawers filled with old linen embroidered with my grandmother's and great grandmother's monograms, I came across a small plastic bag in which were two coat hangers covered in blue wool with a label my mother had written, undoubtedly intended for me: 'Crocheted by Bertha Kaufmann in about 1920'.

So my mother had gone to extreme trouble, at some unknown date to anticipate my future discovery. She knew that one day I would have to carry out this testing, nostalgic, heart-rending task of choosing what must be kept or not kept in the family house. She must have foreseen that moment when she would not be there, and so she had left me this information. She had wanted to draw my attention to it. As if she were addressing me, post mortem, to say to me: 'Look, this is precious, keep it or throw it away, but know where this object came from. It was your great-grandmother who crocheted this. I would like you to keep it in memory of her and of me. Give it to your children and to the children of your children. This is testimony of a long line of women who were dextrous with their hands, attentive about fine linen, caring about their family's well-being, take good care of it, as I have done before you. This is your female inheritance.'

Miraculously preserved from war, moving, exile, this was a part of the trousseaux of several generations of young wives on my mother's side of the family. From among the piles of hand-embroidered linen, my mother had singled out these two coat hangers in their woollen mantle, meticulously crocheted by her maternal grand-mother in the happy years of her childhood. Of all the sheets and linen napery, damask, precious lace, she had said nothing. What could I do about them? Shut them away as she had done in big oak cupboards beautifully scented with lavender which I did not have? Where were the huge tables of long ago, lit by tall candlesticks that cast a welcoming glow over the porcelain services, the silver cutlery and freshly starched napkins? That world had vanished, that way of life no longer existed. I had not been brought up to marry and keep house according to those rules of a bygone age. My ancestors' savoir-faire had not been handed down.

Agnès, Sophie, Julia, Regina, Caroline, Amalia, Bertha, my matriarchs of years gone by, of five, six or seven generations ago, I salute you through your napery and your white sheets. I think of your fate as strong courageous women. You gathered the fruits of life, you passed on life to me, and I, in turn, have passed on life. Don't be angry with me, I am a words-and-paper daughter. Of your trousseaux, I shall keep but a few of the most beautiful pieces in memory of you. Do not ask me to wash these precious fabrics by hand, calender them, starch them, mend tears, darn holes. Your great-great-granddaughter has given up the needle for the fountain pen and laptop.

Cupboards, wardrobes, everything was overflowing with clothes and linen: ironed, folded, put away in even piles, sometimes even slipped into plastic bags and wrapped in tissue paper in little boxes, dozens of pullovers, blouses, camisoles, tank tops, tee-shirts lay there, perhaps still waiting to be worn and admired. They were all autumn colours, colours that my mother loved: from golden brown to light chestnut, from a honeyed orange to camel, to ivory, from russet to very dark brown, with here and there unexpected colours, amaranthine, deep purple or sky blue with contrasting stripes, bright points in precious materials. Everything was impeccable, as though brand-new, laid out like a luxury boutique.

My mother valued distinction and elegance. She was said to have been a revolutionary at twenty, but had always had a weakness for beautiful outfits. In her eyes I was never neat and tidy. As a child my hair was always unruly, the collars of my blouses were never white for long; before the end of the day, or even in the course of a visit, everything would go askew: my socks would wrinkle around my legs and wickedly fall down over my shoes, my shoelaces would undo, the knots were clumsy, my skirt would turn round my waist, my blouse would crease, everything was beyond me, I was a real disaster area.

As for my mother, well, she never had a hair

out of place from the way it was set, her nails were impeccably lacquered, her eyebrows pencilled perfectly, the line in her stockings was always as straight as a die down the back of her legs, her shoes and bag matched and shone with polish. Her outfit was classic, sober: most of the time in monochrome beige, in blue, white or red in spring. My mother dressed with a rather austere, almost rigid elegance, but occasionally she might break this order for an afternoon or evening with an eccentric, home-made ensemble.

Under her distinction lay immoderation; she was a curious mixture of excess and control. She certainly feared her enthusiasms and passions and sought to curb them. Fire burned under the ash. And what she could not bear in herself, she repressed in me: high spirits, disorder, insouciance, sensuality.

In her youth she had learned dressmaking. For several months she lived in Tours as an apprentice seamstress in a fashion house. Her grandmother had been a fashion designer, she had a shop selling her own millinery. My mother kept her passion for fashion throughout her life, which strengthened her bond with her grandmother who had partly brought her up, and for whom my mother felt only tenderness and admiration. She loved telling me that what her hands had fashioned could also be fashioned by others. This was my mother's creed.

I had always seen her sewing. She bought paper patterns and pinned them on to the fabric that she had chosen – silk, wool, muslin, velvet. I loved watching her draw around the pieces of paper with fine white chalk, then cut out the pieces, pin the garment together, and tack it before removing the pins and trying it on for the first time.

Often she would put only half the dress together before trying it on. She would look in the mirror, surrounded with rustling tissue paper, holding her dress-to-be to the hollow of her waist, bending her elbow to see the length of a sleeve, the depth of a pleat, frowning, a few pins with coloured heads sticking from her mouth. Sometimes she would ask me to hitch up a shoulder and slip in a few pins. I would prick myself and cry out and she would tell me off. She would explain to me that professional dressmakers would always have a bit of white linen in their mouth with which to dab the beads of blood that appeared on their fingertips. The dress, the skirt, the almost finished jacket would be completely assembled, and then sewn on the sewing machine in fine solid stitches in silk thread which exactly matched the colour of the fabric. Tone on tone. She would finish her work by making the buttonholes by hand.

I loved watching her make the buttonholes, the loops, slipping small lengths of tape under the straps to hold the bra and prevent it from showing, sewing small pads under the armholes to absorb perspiration so that the wool or silk would not be stained and be left with an unpleasant aureole. For an evening dress she wore once, when she got married, she spent hours and hours, over the course of several weeks, covering it in sequins with iridescent reflections.

Twenty, thirty, forty years later, I stood in front of her open wardrobe and contemplated those dresses that she had sewn by hand with infinite patience, unfailing attentiveness, always ready to undo anything that she did not consider perfect. She was an indefatigable Madame Perfect.

I often surprised her sticking her tongue out

slightly in her effort of concentration. She could not be disturbed. She held her breath as she adjusted, corrected, retraced the curve of an opening or flare, an armhole, cutting a curve to shape, the circle of a décolleté, the line of a lapel, the fall of a skirt. She used marvellous words that no one else used: guipure, smocking, crêpe de chine, piping, lazy daisy, gores, galloons and gimps…

I could follow the evolution of the female silhouette, as though I were in a fashion museum, right through the sixties, seventies, eighties to the end of the century. She had kept everything and the memories flowed, bringing with them the olfactory memory of her perfume: Chanel No 5. It was the perfume of a generation of mothers. I was the child of this mythical bouquet that enveloped Marilyn's radiant nakedness. There, in the shadows of the dark cupboard, I found the little black low-cut dress with the twirling skirt and black lace sleeves that she had worn to a friend's wedding in Berlin in 1970. There was the red woollen body-hugging princess-line dress tailored under the breasts that she used to wear with a wonderful medallion that had belonged to her grandmother and which I dreamed of wearing one day, in my turn. The outfit in pearl-coloured raw silk with its matching blouse, buttoned up and hanging on a wooden hanger snitched from some grand hotel, the orange summer dress that brought back memories of happy summer holidays when I was just a little girl in Saint-Raphaël or at the Foresteria at Torre del Lago-Puccini. And also the silk voile dress as light as breath, the red cashmere frock, the pleated shantung dress, the trouser suit in sea blue raw silk, the richly coloured taffeta skirt, the beige suit, the long damask skirt.

What was I going to do with this wardrobe which was such an intimate testimony of her savoir-faire, that seemed to preserve not only the shape of her body, her gestures, but was a living example of her talent, her very assured taste, her artistic soul? I closed the cupboard, discouraged. I would never have the cynicism either to sell or throw away, or give up to some anonymous woman these dresses hidden away from the passing of time, shielded from old age and illness, marvellously intact, for ever perfectly beautiful.

I let several days go by before I opened the

wardrobe door again and began to take out what had been left under the hanging clothes. Large hastily filled plastic bags contained an endless selection of winter hats, leather handbags dating from the 1940s. Hidden away at the back under a pile of scarves, gloves, shawls, socks and fabric flowers protected in transparent boxes, I discovered a large bag which had belonged to my grandmother. I opened it and stood there stupefied. It contained exactly what the mother of my mother had put there in the last days of her life.

Since her death in February 1979, almost twenty-three years earlier, my own mother had not emptied it; perhaps she had not even opened it, slipping it to the back of the cupboard without being able to touch it. It came back to me that she did not empty the small flat her mother had occupied at the end of her life, she made me do it.

Why had she left me to do it, all on my own, emptying all my grandmother's cupboards? Overcome by this experience I had angrily and somewhat cruelly said to her 'I hope that you will at least put her papers in order'. She had done so. But I still had to make the inventory of my grandmother's bag, such as it had remained at the time of her death. I slipped the catches and half opened it.

There were still sweets inside, stuck to the netting of a white and yellow grocery bag, as though poking out from a fishing net. Sticky but still wrapped in their multicoloured transparent wrappers, the sweets seemed to be waiting to be offered to some nice little children. My grandmother was never without them. She always had some on her in the depths of her pockets or in her handbag, something sweet to give to the children she met. All her life she had been like that, she loved to please, each and everyone. She seduced so many people, everyone except her own daughter. My mother never forgave her for preferring the cinema and tennis to her duties as a mother.

My grandmother made up for it with me. In her mature years she offered me the tenderness that in her youth she had been unable to give her own daughter. For me she was a real softie. She would make me marvellous marbled cakes, succulent vol-au-vents, homemade pasta that she would cut out and dry on the backs of chairs that she kept specially for this purpose in her huge kitchen.

A generous chatterbox, she seemed to me to be like all grandmothers, the opposite of my mother who was demanding, severe and impossible to satisfy. In the raspberry season she would invite me to gather up the greatest possible number of my playmates to come and pick them in her garden. She loved seeing us all smothered in red, and laughing from this abundant harvest, and would encourage us to linger there with her, giving us permission to use her white sheets to make tents, and play with the weights of her brass scales, and dress up in her hats and scarves. I believe it was her blusher and mascara that were the first make up I ever tried.

Her lipstick was called 'Rouge baiser' – red kiss. I spread my mouth with it and invented future scenes of seduction for myself. She was a willing accomplice of my young woman's dreams. It was she who first told me about periods and boys who corner you. I rode my roller skates in front of her house and I still remember a small very blond boy who was a neighbour who pursued me and tried to catch me to cut off my pigtails. My grandmother whom everyone affectionately called Mémée was a highly colourful, lively, nervous sort of person, who spoke very loudly, gesticulating with her hands like an Italian or Spanish woman. I never knew her with white hair – she dyed it till the end of her life and died in her bed with a young lover at her side. I would like to die like her, still in love.

I emptied her bag, piece by piece. Other than the sweets I found there were some sugar cubes and a sugar sachet with a picture of a black cat that was a brand of coffee, a rain hat and numerous photos: her own mother's, her daughter and granddaughter, her gentle-faced sister Irène, taken in 1935, whose ring I have worn for more than twenty years – a sober rectangle of black quartz in the centre of which shines a small diamond. I am very fond of this jewel to which a thousand misadventures have occurred, but which with unfailing fidelity has always found its way back to my finger. On one of these photos you can see me, a long beanpole of nine or ten with legs that have grown too quickly, a slightly daft appearance, a pleated skirt that is too short, a stripy sailor's top, in the company of my behatted smiling grandmother.

We seem delighted to be together beside the

North Sea, accomplices in the way that only grandchildren and their grandparents are.

Miraculously preserved despite the spilt sugar was a drawing that I had given her a few years before her death, an affectionate testimony that had never left her handbag. She had loved me; I hope that I have inherited her vivaciousness, her curiosity, her humour, her sometimes exuberant affection, her talents as a pastry cook and her capacity to bond with no matter whom no matter where. She had a passion for second-hand markets, salesrooms and flea markets. She would hunt for antiques several times a week and had collections of Persian carpets and silver. I shall always regret the little heart-shaped, delicately wrought box that my mother and I encouraged her to resell. She had an eye for things and would bring home small charmless objects in a fever of excitement which after her assiduous cleaning would be restored to their former beauty. She had taught me some bargaining tricks, telling me never to show an initial interest in what my heart was really set on and then I could hope to carry it away at a good price after feigning interest in another object of desire. Basically, what amused her most was human intercourse, conversation, reciprocal games of cunning, the time given to exchange, the value of talking.

I performed difficult feats that my mother had refused to do. Without doubt there exist goodbye gestures to the things that belonged to dead people, just as there are for the dead themselves. The ritual of fire rather than burial in the ground, gifts to the most underprivileged, presents to friends, memories slipped to the back of a drawer, a knick-knack negligently placed on a windowsill, a drawing, a photograph or a letter put back between the pages of a bedside book. Jewellery belonging to the women of the family often undergoes a different fate: it is slipped on fingers, passed over wrists, around necks, on ears, it circulates from one generation to another, from skin to skin. Jewels do not like staying in their box, they come to life and shine in contact with the skin. When she was alive my grandmother had given me her sister's ring, two long necklaces and a small powder compact on a chain, jewellery that I have always gone on wearing, just like the pair of earrings and the bracelets that my mother gave me. But the object that she passed on to me and which is dearest to me, my most precious inheritance though I cannot say why, is a small pair of silver grape scissors.

Bizarrely, for the first time in my life, I began to wear colours that my mother was fond of and that I believed were solely reserved for her. For several days I wore her favourite earrings and one of her scarves. I took home a silk square that recounted Peynets's lovers' trip around the world that she had been given in the 1950s. I remember at the age of four or five I would spend hours, stretched out on my parents' bed, follow-ing the peregrinations of these two pretty travellers, imagining that, when my turn came, in the distant future, I would do the same...'You take me...dear...I shall make myself very small...'

But what was I going to do with the contents of her exceptional wardrobe, with this almost 'haute couture' collection of unique model dresses and suits, hand sewn and signed in the pockets or on the collars, where my mother had attached a label 'Handmade by Mami' with the date the garment was finished added in her handwriting. I could not wear any of these dresses myself, they were not made for me. Then I had an idea: perhaps a Norwegian friend of mine would agree to try some on, just to see.

The trying-on took place several days later and surprised us both beyond what I could have imagined. It was a shock, a revelation. Although she did not look as though she had the same silhouette as my mother, she was much taller and rangier, the clothes, that had been conceived and made for another woman, looked wildly alluring on my friend. She wore them in quite a different way from their originator, they moved marvellously on her. Through her bedazzled expression – like a little girl to whom a fairy had given the clothes of a princess – I was able to render homage to my mother's talent. She savoured every detail, each refinement of the tailoring, the beautiful way a garment hung, an original cut, the movement of a pleat, of a curve, the softness of the fabric, the perfect finishing, invisible to the naked eye. Perhaps I was conscious for the first time of the real work that had gone into this wardrobe of my mother's. One by one, I held out the garments to my friend, who tried them on looking at herself each time in the mirror of the room and in the mirror of my eyes.

We were, one and the other, bewitched in a magic circle. Something unexpected, unhoped for, was in the act of being created. Her childhood dreams were fulfilled, and I accomplished the wish that my mother had not expressed but I had taken from her: to see all the clothes, created and made with love and dexterity, admired and given value, worn with elegance and simplicity.

The same scene was re-enacted many times during the summer. Little by little, the whole collection of clothes changed hands. My friend took them over in her fashion, invented new co-ordinates, new mixtures, she gave them a new life.

A dress does not die.

Orphaned Objects

Things have their secrets,
their legends,
but, if we know how to listen,
they can talk to us.

Barbara Drouot

Objects live several times over, but once passed on to new owners, do they keep any trace of their former life? It is no matter of indifference to imagine them elsewhere, in other hands, for uses that are superimposed on those they previously had. I needed to believe that these objects that had been chosen and cared for by my parents were loved, had effort put into them, were cherished by their new owners. In order to give them away, without feelings of regret or guilt, I wanted to know that they were being used and growing old in the midst of attention. Things are not so different from people or animals. Objects have a soul. I felt as though I were responsible for protecting them from too dismal a fate.

I had already spent hours and hours considering them, allowing myself to be flooded with memories, yet remaining indecisive, not knowing what to do with them, wanting to be separated from them but at the same time wanting to keep them. I clutched them as though saying goodbye, then, wearily, put them in a cardboard box, delaying a decision that was still too heartrending.

On days when I despaired of ever seeing the house empty, I was generous, even prodigious. On days when my courage returned, I pursued my task like a worker bee, with my head placed firmly on my shoulders. I threw things away parsimoniously, gave away advisedly, sold for the best price, and brought home with me everything that could be found a place there: books in my library, crockery in my cupboards, scent bottles in my bathroom, pictures on the walls.

But my house was not expandable. I could not play at communicating vessels: emptying from one side to fill the other. Was my healthy aggression becoming blunted? I told myself that objects must circulate. They will live a long time after us, faded and torn, with no one to mourn them. They properly belong to no one, they are confided to us for a time. They must continue their rounds. Each in turn must enjoy them.

Occasional visitors, casting a discreet glance around them, assessing the task that I still had to accomplish, could not help but regard me with pity and commiseration and say, ' Oh, you poor dear,' which left me no chance to delude myself. Inwardly I protested, convincing myself of their complete insensitivity towards my treasures of the past. Every individual is attached only to their own trinkets, knick-knacks and trifles, other people's are of no interest. It's always easy to throw away something that has no sentimental value for yourself. But separating yourself from your own memories isn't separating, it's amputating. Detachment is rarely instantaneous. It demands a longer internal metamorphosis, patient work, and constant testing.

My feelings that wavered between nostalgia and exhaustion varied from one moment to the next. On some days I carried home entire cases of books (God, paper is so heavy), moved boxes of linen and crockery (for when I would get a house in the country), folded clothes to give away, threw away what had to be thrown, put to one side what I wanted to try to sell.

On other days I was overcome with discouragement, immobilised by paralysis. I was annoyed with my parents for not thinking of doing this great clear-out themselves.

I was hoping to sell furniture, cumbersome objects that could have no room at my house, so great was my humiliation when I found no one to give me a good price. Had my parents miscalculated the value or quality of their choices? Had the market changed in the intervening years? I was vexed on their behalf. I abandoned the idea of getting money for them, I gave them away. The pleasure of giving was unambivalent.

Once again I turned to the boxes filled with memories. Mine were mixed with theirs. The address of a hotel in Calella Palfrugell where I had spent holidays when I was seven or eight brought back the image of a young boy I had liked. He was as lively as a lightning flash, voluble, mischievous, a bit of a bandit, and I chose him from among all the children with whom I played. When we went for a walk once, alone among the pines, quite intimidated by the fact that we were so far away from our friends, I put a small stone on the path, promising myself that I would never forget it. The stone and the boy have remained in my memory, suddenly reawakened in singular circumstances. I can no longer remember the boy's name, but it is not impossible that subconsciously he has guided my choice of the people I have fallen in love with.

Old tourist brochures, out-of-date magazines, obsolete telephone messages, I happily shoved everything that fell into my hands into big rubbish bags. It was a splendid day. No pain, no guilt held me back. The shelves in the loft were at last empty. I felt unalloyed joy. But when I saw a big red and green box, my enthusiasm was suspended.

Carefully placed inside were dozens of paper napkins from cafés and restaurants from the entire world. I wanted to throw them away immediately, then hesitated just for a moment before examining them more carefully. At the bottom of each my mother's fine, firm and free handwriting could clearly be seen, imprinting on these anodyne bits of paper an unexpectedly true, light, and persistent emotion.

Vacillating, and enclosed in the small dark loft, while the brilliant sun was blazing outside, I considered the strangeness of this collection, the absurdity of my situation. Through what infernal powers was I, like Persephone, being kept underground: separated from life, from all light? It was at this moment that the idea of writing these pages came to me.

Goffered papers, with imprints, with red and white gingham designs like authentic cloth napkins, marked with exotic names of faraway places, slogans, attractive or ridiculous drawings, I brought them all back to my work table. Rather like a list by the avant-garde novelist George Perec or an inventory by Prévert, you were listed one after the other. I could not consign you to the void without noting down the strange rosary you formed:

Ventimiglia 29 August 1988 Casa del Caffe, Orleans, 2 March 1983, Les Musardises, pâtisserie devoted exclusively to fine butter,

Bruges, 18 June 1983, Brasserie lyrique,
Copenhagen, 15 November 1981, Hotel
Scandinavia.
The Scaramouche in Amsterdam,
The Casanova in Milan,
A Japanese restaurant in Hamburg,
A Greek bar in Rotterdam . . .

a geography without head or tail, like those
drawings in dots which have a meaning once all
the dots have been joined up.

These things occupy the imagination of those
who keep a special meaningful place for them,
inextricable from the sometimes labyrinthine
bonds that bind them together. They cannot
escape the aura of mystery with which we endow
them. As alien to the passion that gave these
paper napkins life for their departed owners I
could only meet them through gently touching
these objects. Their journeys will remain
unknown.

What would my occasional visitors have
thought had they surprised me lifting up these
napkins one by one and writing them in my
inventory rather than throwing them into the

wastepaper basket. That I was a bit touched? That I would still be here in a year's time? That I should apply a bit more method and less emotion? That I should not keep everything, nor even look at everything before throwing it away? That what I was doing bordered on the ridiculous?

Perhaps it was my own way of paying the price for – dare I say it? – a more and more vivid sensation of joie-de-vivre.

I did not want emptying my parents' house to become synonymous with abandonment and anonymity. I had not called in someone to clear the house, one of those horrible predators who send you their condolences the day after the funeral and suggest at the same time that you allow them to enter your distress and your house, to relieve you in the twinkling of an eye of the contents of all your memories: trinkets with hidden treasures (of course, they do not present themselves ingenuously), old scraps of iron, rusted tools and the rustic copper pots which will be good for creating the farmhouse look in antique shop windows, the old telephone where you have to turn the heavy black metal dial, which will soon become the in-thing, the tools that used to produce good workmanship, work well done, the appropriateness between gesture and function, the hand and the material – which today no one wants any more because they are synonymous with work and patience and the catchphrase is assuredly: instant pleasure – but that the secondhand dealers will soon be selling for a fortune to feed the dreams of 'postmodernist' buyers. The old vinyl records that have already been fought over, the outdated road maps, old tourist travel guides – almost histories, for the present has become infatuated with a very recent past and calls it *vintage*: fluorescent pink and orange armchairs of the sixties, low sideboards on feet 'Guaranteed a Knoll copy'; plates of Scandinavian design, flying saucer ashtrays, round pouffes, drapes with psychedelic patterns, peace and love Venus of India jewels and clothes… A whole load of bric-à-brac with which I had no idea what to do, but which I had not the heart to jettison.

There was a mixture of every epoch at the back of the loft and in different cellars in the house. I would have liked to gather a few people so that they could each turn something to their advantage, choose something, find a suitable match, fit an odd lid on to an incomplete pot, or box, put their hand on a rare antique that they had long sought. Dozens and dozens of objects from sales, gifts, the chances that life offers were in a state of disinheritance, left to themselves. No one would handle them lovingly any more, nor dust them, nor covet them with a jealous protective glance

Objects become orphans too. They need adoptive parents, new friends, new exclusive and furiously jealous owners who will take care of them. Objects suffer from being useless, abandoned, idle.

How, for example, could I throw away keys that belonged to nothing? I no longer knew the locks – of doors or suitcases – I could not resolve to get rid of them just like that: as if in some part of the world, a door or a suitcase was waiting to be delivered from its prison by a forgotten key. I did not want to condemn them to an everlasting wait.

It was imperative that I found an enthusiast for my five-footed sheep: a collector of matchboxes who would be bowled over by some examples dating from the 1950s, a lover of old cameras, an antique dealer in compasses, inkwells, penholders and desk *matériel* before the information era, or, by contrast, someone who was looking for early models of computers.. A DIY fan for soldering irons, wrecking bars, screws, nails, burins, various pairs of pincers, scissors and spanners of every kind. A patented dressmaker who always wanted at hand fifteen shades of blue or beige thread, masses of pins, needles for every type of fabric from cotton to leather to sail canvas, professional scissors, patterns and multicolour samples of materials, offcuts of cloth or lining material 'which might always come in handy'.

Where could I find someone who wanted to learn Russian (a great choice of methods), *the* collector in search of numbers of a Swiss literary magazine, *La Guilde du Livre*, between 1947 and 1964, a collector of perfume samples, but also solitary gloves, socks with no twins, and a complete panoply of suncreams bought more than fifteen years ago at least, without counting the male or female who would love to acquire every possible brand of electric razor, bars of soap from hotels around the entire world, travelling toothbrushes, international bottles of alcohol, diaries in real leather, miniature pocket calculators, cake moulds of every shape, sugar tongs, and tongs for asparagus (who could have invented them or used them?), small silver spoons still in their presentation velvet case and other presents accumulated over the years that had never been opened? Not to mention the collection of Camembert lids, books on mushrooms, hundreds of freezer boxes, thousands of buttons, hundreds of thousands of paper handkerchiefs and millions of small nails.

But what should I do with the family photos where one has forgotten who they are, who live on without names at the bottom of a cardboard box, orphans not of ancestors but of descendants capable of naming them (this undoubtedly is a fate that awaits us all), of whom no one could note on the back of the faded photo the short name by which they were known?

No one either to wear those out-of-date clothes, old-fashioned sunglasses – unless the fashion comes back into favour, but it won't come back when one needs it to – those stretch ski pants, ski boots in leather that is so stiff and heavy that I wonder any human foot had ever been able to bear them without protesting at each step. Who wants the cassette recorders with round tapes, those things for viewing slides, cocktail mixers, plates with compartments for peanuts, numerous pepper grinders, collections of sugars in old-fashioned sweet jars, plastic spice jars on a turntable, Cinzano bottle openers, cheese picks with a little pig on the end? To whom should I offer the four canisters labelled Flour, Sugar, Biscuits, Coffee, the cut-glass crystal bowls beside the beer mugs, the small wooden barrels, aluminium butter dishes, plates for all occasions, piles of napkins, serviettes, table sets in cotton, linen, straw, lace and polyester? Who would rejoice to receive these vodka glasses, whisky glasses, Burgundy glasses, cognac glasses, lemonade or port glasses, incomplete Champagne flutes and goblets, ice bucket, ice tongs, coffee thermos, primus stove, pocket torches, bottle openers, olive wood salad bowls, empty picture frames, beach bags, garden tools, watch bracelets minus the watches?

And five kilos of bits of candle, who would

ever want these? In contrite heaps in the bottom of numerous biscuit boxes, long and slim, thick-set and squat, these pieces of candle of every colour of the rainbow justify the French expression: 'candle-end economy'.

I did not know whether to laugh or cry. Tenderness won over derision. I took home those candles which had burned at their table and let them shine on mine. I loved lighting all those lights, not throwing anything away before I had watched them slowly melt and burn out by themselves.

Why had I gone throughout so briskly until now? Why should I now suddenly allow myself to be weakened by the smallest, least important bit of string, wax, paper, fabric?

Chaos

She experienced that sense of voluptuousness
that comes to you when you destroy through cleaning,
and see the emptiness taking the place of objects.
Henry de Montherlant

Stop! Enough! *Basta così!* Time to throw away, throw away, and, more significantly, throw away without looking. Enough of cheap sentiment. Time to gaily throw away pages upon pages of old paper into large bins, fingers black with dust and irritated throat. Time to throw away boxes that have no definite use, books falling to bits, old electrical appliances, worn out, faded, dried out, rotting objects of absolutely no interest, this whole mess of assorted wrecks.

Time to bid farewell to our past. All the familiar things that we once loved are no more than

cumbersome old-fashioned stuff. We must separate ourselves from them, joyfully. Celebrate the
victory of life over death.

Taking possession of our parents' treasures,
rich and poor, makes us odious, pitilessly rapa-
cious pirates. However, the house must be empty.
Visibly.

I was very afraid of being swallowed up under
the flood of furniture, objects and archives that
never seemed to grow smaller, in fact quite the
opposite. The house had never been in such a
state of disorder when my parents were alive.
There was a ramshackle mass of disparate things
around me, on the chairs, the floor, in boxes, on
the stairs, the windowsills, beds, tables, kitchen
sink, absolutely everywhere. A real flea market,
with everything out on display.

I found it impossible to stay for more than an
hour or an hour and a half in this pigsty. I could-
n't do one thing at a time, I would spread myself
around, often changing rooms, working away
sometimes on a bookcase shelf in the drawing
room, sometimes on one or two shelves of a
kitchen cupboard or on a drawer in the desk, as if
it were less of an ordeal not to impose any

systematic method. What put an end to each visit was the increasingly oppressive sensation that I had used up all the emotional energy I possessed by turning the knife in the wound of memory.

Before leaving the place, undermined by the impression that I would never reach the end in such a battlefield, I would look here and there around me for a collection of objects whose collective fate would be easy to decide. Not one single thing at a time, which took ages to evaluate, turn over and over in my hands, but a whole drawer, a whole section of books, an unsorted entirety. How wonderful it would be to sever it in one brief definitive phrase: For the Red Cross. To be thrown away. To the sales rooms. To take home with me.

Is inheriting not a choice, making decisions with sovereign power?

In this mood, I particularly liked giving away. Giving on the spur of the moment, without reflecting, having confidence in my intuition, feeling that such and such a black vase decorated with gilt flowers would suit that person, and that simple bowl the other... Pairing off things and people. Playing the matchmaker. I liked giving and I liked that little bit of emptiness that followed. I could not afford to prevaricate, hesitate. Everything had to be settled in an instant. This was a moment of grace, an unusual exchange: I received by giving. I gave in order to receive. I was myself and I was the other person. I transformed my inheritance into a multiplicity of gifts.

A coffee maker, a magnifying glass, a telephone, curtains, nut crackers, a collection of pipes, a Mexican hat, a plant, a drill, a jigsaw, a series of pencil sharpeners, a toaster, an entire box of Champagne glasses in cut glass.

In giving, I was not the person who gave, but the person who received the gift: a first camera to a very young little girl, a fur coat to my sister-in-law, a big calendar of reproductions of Magritte to a friend who was moving to a new flat. I thanked him on the same occasion for accepting the round table with six blue chairs from the dining room, the orange divan, the bed and wardrobe in light wood, the two bedheads in the same wood, and a thousand other household items, among them the big green plant and the made-to-measure kitchen units. So one day I would have the pleasure of seeing these familiar objects again in their second or third life.

Sometimes things found new surprising partners: like the big TV set, the picture of which after a fall had become blue on the right side and no one wanted it any more, I gave it to an old blind woman who couldn't watch television but listened to it and was very happy with the result. The dressing table with the big mirror found a new place in a room of an Indian Muslim family who immediately artistically veiled the mirror.

Giving is a great happiness. What I was offering was not an object. The object is a vehicle, a pretext, it transmits assurance, confidence. I was giving what I had not received: my parents had never let me have anything without an accompanying warning : 'Be careful.' 'Don't break it'. 'Don't spoil it'. 'Don't throw it away'. 'Above all, don't use it your way. It's not really yours, it's still ours. We're not giving you this object, we're lending it to you, slightly against our will. Don't behave like yourself with it, but as we would, which is something you're obviously incapable of, since you have two left hands.'

Were objects, in their eyes, more important than their daughter? The maniacal care with which they surrounded them made me react the opposite way, making them, in spite of myself, right. I would have so much loved them to invite me to use things freely, so that it was not an object that they were giving me but its enjoyment: 'This is for you. Use it how you want, in your own way, we do not mistrust you in any way, there are no restrictions, we don't doubt that what you do with it will suit you (it is you who count and not this object), experiment with it. You can mess it up, break it, throw it away, lose it, it's not important. Enjoy it.'

I looked for students who as yet had almost nothing and needed practically everything. I suggested to them that they took away everything they liked. Overwhelmed but delighted, they embarked on the disorder of armchairs, sofas, chairs, stools, punch bowls, cheese dishes, an Australian boomerang, mattress, cushions, table cloths, candlesticks, lamps, an African lance, salad shakers and books for amusement: *The Art of Folding Napkins to Decorate the Table, How to Read your Future in the Cards,* or *A 1,000*

Helpful Hints to Make your Life Better, and so
on…and on…and on...

They went away loaded and happy.

I felt light.

Journey through Bereavement

This book has been vital to me as evidence. Assailed by emotions that were diffuse, ambiguous, violent, sometimes incompatible with each other, the words sprang up by themselves. Writing captured this boiling wave of emotions. The writing was born out of bereavement and offered it a refuge. A place to shelter before confronting new discomforting waves that had to be contained.

The experience of grief is lived through in solitude. It is not only pain and regret. Aggression, anger, rage are present too. It is difficult to admit: the dead and their offspring only supposed that they would awaken tender, respectful, agreeable feelings. All excess would be banished. How deluded can we be.

The psychology of it is much more mixed. It is

made of imprecise gestures, of incessant turnings and returnings, it is never smooth, pure, univocal. Around death and birth (illness, lovers' meetings and separation etc.) feelings press so acutely that they destabilise us, turn us upside down through their powerfulness and disorder. These are moments of intense inner reshaping. They lead us to explore ways that we have never trodden, reopen badly marked routes, to dare to cross obstacles which appeared impossible to confront. They lead us beyond ourselves.

Becoming an orphan, even late in life, demands a new way of thinking. We talk of the work of bereavement, it might also be called a rite of passage, a metamorphosis.

The sharp ridges of early grief become blunted, stolidity and protestations give way to a slow acceptance of reality. Despondency wells up with moments of emptiness, absence, tumult. Later a sadness infuses us, imprinted with gentleness. Inside us a tender hurt envelops the image of the absent one. Death is coiled up in us. This path has no short cuts. There is no escape from it. Death belongs to life, life encapsulates death.

Emptying the house of our departed ones

exacerbates the experience of mourning, accentuates all its characteristics. As in a chemical analysis, each task reveals the smallest particular of our attachments, our conflicts, our disillusions. Even those bereaved who call in the house clearance people cannot economise in their memory or in their grief. Each one of us is plunged into them. But there is a time for sorrow and a time for joy.

Persephone, having passed the winter months underground, returns to the light of the sun, she sows the fields and the orchards. Flowers grow and fruit again. It is not good to imprison yourself in melancholy.

I do not want to put a final full stop to this book